ROLE

an exploration of positive influence

"Empower Girls;
Change the World."

-Dr. Eboni Bell

Dream Nation Mentor Book Series

Scan me

Our Mission

The mission of Dream Girl Box is to encourage girls to Dream Big by practicing the habit of goal setting and the core values of:

COURAGE
CONFIDENCE
CREATIVITY
&
GOOD CHARACTER

n our Dream Nation Mentor Books, girls reflect on
hese core values through self-exploration,
ctivities, and challenges that can be completed
ndividually or with a parent or mentor.

Acknowledgements

Thsi

This book is dedicated to Amanda Gorman,
who is a great role model for girls.
She displays poise, confidence, beauty,
humility, and artistic ability.

Thank you for showing girls and women,
all over the globe that they can be classy,
beautiful, and intelligent.

Contents

Let's Get Into It

Dan

Why do we need positive influences in our lives? We need positive influences to help shape us into who we can be. When we see what we can achieve, it makes our goals more acheivable.

What is a role model? A role model is an influential person who inspires you to live a purposeful and meaningful life. We want to have positive role models who influence us to learn, to grow, and to reach our full potential in life.

In this book, we will explore role models and why it's important to have positive influences and examples as we follow our dreams and achieve our life goals.

We need each other!

Let's Explore Role Models

Let's Define It: Role Model

In your own words, describe what a role model is. Use some descriptive words to tell us what a role model is.

Essential Questions

In this mentor book, we will explore these essential questions. Our goal is for you to be able to clearly answer these questions and share with others around you.

*You will answer these questions at the end of the book.

Q #1

What is a positive influence, and why is it important to have positive influences in your life?

Q #2

What is a role model, and why is it beneficial to have people you look up to?

What I Do

What qualities do you look for in a positive influence? Fill the stars with positive attributes.

What I Do

What indicates that something or someone is NOT a positive influence in your life?

CAUTION

CAUTION

CAUTION

What I've Seen

Have you ever witnessed a negative influence in a show, a movie, or on social media?

Who was it, and why do you think their behaviors were negative?

What I've Seen

Who do you consider to be a role model in your life? Think about family members, teachers, coaches, friends, or even characters.

Family Role Model

Community Role Model

Famous Role Model

What I Want To Do

Do you feel that it's important to be a positive influence in the lives of others? Explain your answer.

What I Want To Do

What kind of role model would you like to be for your peers, friends, and younger family members?

List some characteristics you can build on.

A Role Model Is...

Overcoming The Obstacles

Sometimes being a role model is hard.

Do you think having influence and being someone people look up to can be hard? Do we expect our role models to be perfect? List some reasons why it may be hard to be a role model.

Dream Challenge

Create a video about why it's important to have positive influences in your life. Then, talk about one of your role models. Post it on social media to inspire others and tag @dreamgirlbox.

My Role Model Affirmation

We are going to create a statement about our character and what it means to be a good person.

Example: I want to be a nice, caring, and compassionate person.

My best quality is

_____

_____,

and I will use it to influence

_____

_____

12

Okay, Dream Girls Let's Have Fun With It

Here is where you write freely!

Don't second guess or doubt your thoughts and feelings.

Just express yourself.

My Journal

Prompt: Why do you need positive influences
and role models in your life?

My Journal

Prompt: My biggest role model is:

Draw a picture of one of your role models.

My Journal

Challenge: Ask a parent or trusted adult who
their role models were as a child, and why.
 Take some notes on the conversation.

My Journal

Prompt: Who are some of the role models in your community?

My Journal

Prompt: Do you think your role models will be remembered in history? If so, what will they be remembered for?

Have Fun With It

Activity: Build the ideal role model by giving her admirable characteristics.

considerate

Have Fun With It

Activity: What makes you a good role model?
Introduce yourself as a role model.

HELLO
my name is

Have Fun With It

Activity: Write a characteristic of a positive influence using the letters in the words "role model."

See the example below.

R eal and authentic

O

l

e

M

o

d

e

l

Have Fun With It

Activity: Let's see if you can get bingo with women in history. Put an X on the women you know or look up to. You may have to do some research.

Women in History

Ella Fitzgerald	Katherine Johnson	**Ruby Bridges**	Shirley Chisholm
RBG	Serena Williams	**Kamala Harris**	**Ciara**
Mae	Michelle Obama	**Amelia Earhart**	**Rosa Parks**
Marie Curie	**Oprah**	**Hillary Clinton**	Sandra Day O'Connor

myfreebingocards.com

22

Have Fun With It

Activity: Make a plan/list on how you will be a good influence on those around you.

Have Fun With It

Color this powerful statement with crayons, colored pencils, or markers.

Have Some Fun
With These
Coloring Pages

Design the Dream Girl Squad
Characters by Dr. Eboni Bell

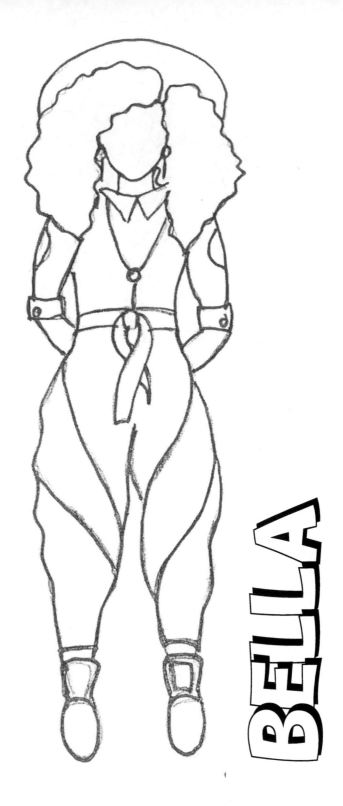

BELLA

PARIS

Essential Questions

Okay! Let's review. You've explored positive influences and role models. It's time to answer our essential questions! Go for it!

Q #1

What is a positive influence, and why is it important to have positive influences in your life?

Q #2

What is a role model, and why is it beneficial to have people to look up to?

Congratulations,
Dream Girl!
You took the journey.

Remember:
Choose your role models
carefully, and try to surround
yourself with positive influences.

Made in the USA
Middletown, DE
17 April 2021

37129110R00022